NEW HAMPSHIRE PATRIOTS

Their Lives, Contributions, and Burial Sites

JOE FARRELL • LAWRENCE KNORR • JOE FARLEY

SUNBURY
PRESS

Mechanicsburg, PA USA

Published by Sunbury Press, Inc.
Mechanicsburg, Pennsylvania

SUNBURY
PRESS
www.sunburypress.com

For information about special discounts for bulk purchases, please contact Sunbury Press Orders Dept. at (855) 338-8359 or orders@sunburypress.com.

To request one of our authors for speaking engagements or book signings, please contact Sunbury Press Publicity Dept. at publicity@sunburypress.com.

FIRST SUNBURY PRESS EDITION: June 2025

Set in Adobe Garamond | Interior design by Crystal Devine | Cover by Lawrence Knorr | Edited by the authors.

Publisher's Cataloging-in-Publication Data
Names: Farrell, Joe, author | Farley, Joe, author | Knorr, Lawrence, author.
Title: New Hampshire patriots : their lives, contributions, and burial sites / Joe Farrell Lawrence Knorr Joe Farley.
Description: First trade paperback edition. | Mechanicsburg, PA : Sunbury Press, 2025.
Summary: The individuals from New Hampshire who played prominent roles in the founding of the USA are detailed.
Identifiers: ISBN 979-8-88819-212-2 (softcover).
Subjects: HISTORY / United States / Revolutionary Period (1775-1800) | BIOGRAPHY & AUTOBIOGRAPHY / Political.

Designed in the USA
0 1 1 2 3 5 8 13 21 34 55

For the Love of Books!

Contents

Introduction

Though a small state, New Hampshire played a large role in the American Revolution. The Pine Tree Riot of 1772 was a precursor to other protests against British authority, such as the Boston Tea Party, which occurred just two years later. What would later be known as The Granite State was the first to declare independence from Great Britain, six months before the Declaration of Independence was adopted in Philadelphia on July 4, 1776. Thus, the motto for New Hampshire, harkening back to the Revolution, has been "Live free or die."

The first patriot in this book is someone who did *not* sign any of the founding documents of our nation, nor did he fight for our independence. Meshech Weare, known as "The Father of New Hampshire," was in his sixties when hostilities began. Rather than taking up arms or traveling to Philadelphia as a Congressman, Weare focused on his state and led the independence movement, devising the first state constitution and serving as the first governor throughout the Revolution.

Other great patriots from New Hampshire served as governors. John Langdon did so four times! John Sullivan and Josiah Bartlett also served as the chief executives of the state.

New Hampshire also gave birth to several dynamic military leaders. The best known was probably Major General John Sullivan and his brutal eponymous expedition in 1779 against the Native Americans who were allied with the crown. Major General John Stark is said to have coined the state motto and was dubbed "The Hero of Bennington" for his leadership in the victory there against the British. Brigadier General William Whipple was a key contributor to the victory at the Battle of Saratoga. Nicholas Gilman and Nathanial Folsom also fought in the Revolution.

As Continental Congressmen, several New Hampshire leaders signed the founding documents of our nation. Nathaniel Folsom and John Sullivan signed the Continental Association. Matthew Thornton, William Whipple, and Dr. Josiah Bartlett signed the Declaration of

Independence. John Wentworth Jr. and Dr. Josiah Barlett signed the Articles of Confederation. Nicholas Gilman and John Langdon signed the US Constitution. All told, twelve great Patriots from New Hampshire fill the pages of this book. While they are not close to the total of all persons who sacrificed or contributed in some way to the cause, they represent those most prominent or famous or who gave the most.

Please enjoy the retelling of our founding through the brief biographies of these citizens of New Hampshire. Always remember: "Poor is the nation that has no heroes, but poorer still is the nation that having heroes, fails to remember and honor them." (attributed to Marcus Tullius Cicero)

Lawrence Knorr, Ph.D.
June 2025

Meshech Weare
(1713 – 1786)

The Father of New Hampshire

Old Brookside Cemetery
Hampton Falls, New Hampshire

First Governor

Mesech Weare did not sign any of the founding documents of the United States, nor did he serve in the Continental Army or New Hampshire Militia during the American Revolution. Weare, who was in his sixties when the Revolution began, was the political leader of the first state to declare independence, as chairman of the Committee of Safety and then governor.

Weare was born in New Parish (now Seabrook), New Hampshire, on June 16, 1713, a son of Deacon Nathaniel Weare and his second wife, Mary Waite Weare. Weare was the youngest of fourteen children.

Weare attended Harvard College intending to enter the Congregational ministry, like his father. He graduated in 1735 but changed his career plans when he married Elizabeth Shaw, the daughter of Deacon Samuel Shaw and Mary Tuck Shaw of Hampton Falls, in 1738. The couple purchased land and became farmers, living in a house built by her father in 1737.

Weare began his political career as a town moderator in 1739. Not long after, his first marriage ended with the unexpected passing of Elizabeth in 1743. This couple had one son, Samuel Weare, born 1741,

The Albany Congress of 1754

and one daughter, Mary, born 1743. It appears Elizabeth's death was related to childbirth.

Weare next married Mehitable Wainwright, the daughter of John and Ann Wainwright, in 1746. This couple had seven children, including Nathaniel, Elizabeth, Abigail, Richard, Hannah, Thomas, and Redford. Son Richard Weare later served as captain of the second company of the 3rd New Hampshire Regiment during the Revolution.

During this time, Weare farmed and raised his family. He also studied law books passed down to him from his father and grandfather, who had been lay judges in the provincial court.

Through 1774, Weare served in various local political positions, including selectman and representative to the New Hampshire Assembly from Hampton Falls. Weare was elected Speaker of the Assembly three times and clerk for eight years.

In 1754, Weare was a delegate to the Albany Congress on behalf of New Hampshire, responding to Ben Franklin's call to "Join or Die," made famous in a cartoon of the time. While the discussions focused on maintaining an alliance with the Iroquois before the French and Indian

Benjamin Franklin Join or Die cartoon from 1754

War, this marked the first time the various colonies considered uniting for a common cause.

In September 1772, Weare was one of four judges empaneled to hear the trial of the participants in what became known as the Pine Tree Riot. In those days, white

Pine Tree Riot flag

pine trees were prized for being tall, straight, and strong and were preferred for ship masts. The Royal Navy valued the white pines of New Hampshire, and they were often selected and marked as the property of the crown. A law passed in 1708 allotted all such trees for this purpose. Early in 1772, several millers were caught using marked pines without permission. The sheriff and his deputy arrested the perpetrators and attempted to spend the night at the Pine Tree Tavern. During the night, angry men with soot-covered faces burst into the room and beat the sheriff and deputy with pine switches, injuring them and sending them to the street, where they found their horses' ears, manes, and tails clipped. The officials rode off, angered and embarrassed. Later, a posse led by a local colonel arrived to arrest the rioters, who had taken to the woods.

Weare Memorial in Hampton Falls, New Hampshire

The men were rounded up and brought before the court. The lenient judges, while finding the men guilty of assault, released them with only light fines.

As the relationship with the crown deteriorated, Weare was among the leaders of the rebellion in New Hampshire. In early 1776, he led the effort to create a constitution for New Hampshire. On January 5, 1776, this state constitution was adopted, making New Hampshire the first state to declare independence from Great Britain.

The new constitution established a Committee of Safety to oversee the state's military and civil affairs when the Assembly was not in session. After a brief respite, Weare chaired this committee throughout the American Revolution until a new constitution was adopted in 1784.

Weare's grave

During the Revolutionary War period, Weare, in addition to chairing the Committee of Safety, served as chief justice of the state's Superior Court, the highest judicial office in the state.

In 1784, a new constitution was established for New Hampshire, formalizing the chief executive role as President of New Hampshire. Weare was the first to fill this role, holding the office from June 15, 1784, until June 1, 1785. For this

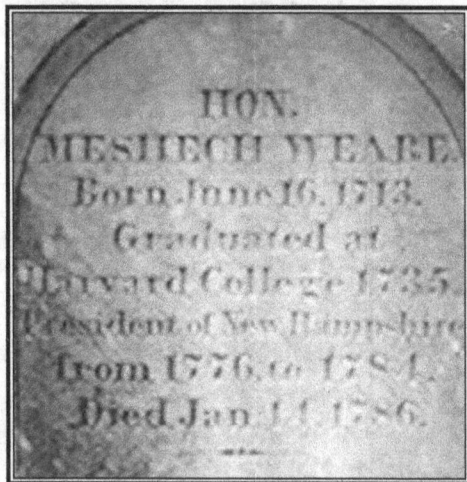

Weare inscription

service and his earlier roles, Weare has been dubbed "The Father of New Hampshire."

Meschech Weare died on January 14, 1786, only months after retiring as governor. He was laid to rest at the Old Brookside Cemetery in Hampton Falls, New Hampshire.

A memorial to Weare was erected in the town square of Hampton Falls. His home is on the National Register of Historic Places. It had been visited by George Washington, James Monroe, and Marquis de Lafayette.

The nearby town of Weare, New Hampshire, was named for him in 1764.

Ethan Allen
(1738 – 1789)

Leader of the Green Mountain Boys

Buried at Green Mountain Cemetery,
Burlington, Vermont.

———————

Ethan Allen is a Revolutionary War hero who was a general in the Continental Army best known as the founder of the famous Green Mountain Boys. He is also known for his tireless and controversial effort to make Vermont independent from Britain, other colonies, and perhaps even from the U.S.

———————

Allen was born in Litchfield, Connecticut, on January 21, 1738, the first born to Joseph and Mary Allen. The family moved to Cornwall, and the Allens had seven more children, five boys and two girls. He began studies under a minister in the nearby town of Salisbury and hoped to gain admission to Yale. That plan was changed when his father died in 1755. He volunteered for militia service during the French and Indian War but saw no action and returned to Cornwall. He met and married Mary Brownson after a short courtship and took part ownership with his brother Heman in an iron furnace in Salisbury. There he bought a small farm and kept developing his iron business. The marriage was an unhappy one. They had five children, two of whom survived to adulthood. Mary died in 1783.

During his time in Salisbury, Allen met Thomas Young, a doctor. They had common interests in philosophy and political theory and decided to

Ethan Allen

collaborate on a book. Young had convinced Allen to become a Deist, i.e., the philosophical position that rejects revelation as a source of divine knowledge and asserts that reason and observation of the natural world are sufficient to determine the existence of god. The book was intended as an attack on organized religion. They worked on it until 1764, when Young moved away, taking the manuscript with him.

In the late 1760s, New Hampshire Governor Benning Wentworth sold land grants west of the Connecticut River. Allen bought grants for about 1000 acres. New York had issued land grants to much of the same land, and the dispute rose to the attention of the New York Supreme Court in 1770. New York won the suit, and Wentworth's grants were declared fraudulent. After the trial, Allen met with other grant holders at Catamount Tavern in Bennington. At this meeting, the settlers formed a militia group to defend their land. They called themselves The Green Mountain Boys and chose Allen as their leader. For the next four years, they fought against New York authorities to keep their land. The New York legislature branded Allen and others as outlaws and offered a reward for their capture.

It was well known throughout New England that there were cannon and artillery at the British forts at Ticonderoga and Crown Point. Following the Battles of Lexington and Concord, a Connecticut militia asked Allen if he and his men would help them capture the forts. He agreed, and the Green Mountain Boys joined 60 men from Massachusetts and Connecticut in a meeting in Bennington on May 2. They planned a dawn raid for May 10. Not long after the Connecticut expedition was launched, the Massachusetts Committee of Safety launched its own expedition with Benedict Arnold in command. On the afternoon of May 9, they met, and Arnold asserted his right to command. The men refused to follow Arnold, and privately Allen and Arnold reached a deal that they would both lead the attack.

The British at Ticonderoga and Crown Point were not aware that war had broken out and were not expecting an attack of any kind. On May 10, 1775, Allen, Arnold, and the Green Mountain Boys stormed the fort at Ticonderoga and captured it with almost no resistance.

The victorious Americans quickly made plans for a strike against Crown Point. Led by Captain Seth Warner, a detachment of the Green Mountain Boys captured the small garrison there. The capture of Fort Ticonderoga and Crown Point proved to be important in the Revolutionary War because it secured protection from the British to the north and provided vital cannon for the colonial army.

When the Continental Congress found out about the capture of the fort, there was concern that it may have ruined any chance at reconciliation with Britain. Congress asked Allen to take the cannon and artillery to the southern end of Lake George so that inventory could be taken. Allen refused the request and argued that removing the weapons from the fort would leave the fort defenseless and leave the colonists in the western territories vulnerable to attack. As long as the cannon and artillery remained at the fort, they could be used to control traffic on Lake Champlain.

The cannon and artillery from Ticonderoga were eventually retrieved by Henry Knox and taken to Boston, where they were used to fortify Dorchester Heights and other areas around the city. Once Dorchester Heights was fortified, the British were forced to evacuate Boston.

On June 22, Allen and Seth Warner appeared before Congress in Philadelphia, where they argued for the inclusion of the Green Mountain

Boys in the Continental Army. Congress agreed to establish a regiment of the Green Mountain Boys and agreed to pay them army rates for their service at Ticonderoga. When the regiment met, they held a vote to determine command. Seth Warner was elected to lead the regiment. He was viewed as a more stable and quieter choice than Allen.

Allen took the rejection in stride and wasted no time in joining Brigadier General Richard Montgomery's invasion of Canada. Operating an independent command ahead of the main body, he botched an attack on Montreal and was captured on September 25. He spent the next two and a half years as a British prisoner, enduring harsh conditions in British castles, New York City jails, and on prison ships. Allen was the type of Yankee the British loved to hate. He was a natural-born leader, brilliant, fearless, crude, bullheaded, arrogant, impulsive, egotistical, confrontational, physically imposing, and principled. General Prescott, the military governor of Montreal, put Allen in irons for 30 days and, with great fanfare, sent him to London to be executed. He arrived at Falmouth, England, after crossing under filthy conditions and was imprisoned in Pendennis Castle, Cornwall. In the meantime, Prescott was captured trying to escape Montreal. King George, fearing for Prescott's fate, decreed that American prisoners should be sent back to America and treated as prisoners of war.

Meanwhile, in January 1777, Vermont declared its independence from Great Britain and land claims from New York and New Hampshire to become the Republic of Vermont, which existed for fourteen years. Though an ally to the American colonies, the Continental Congress did not recognize them, referring to them as "The New Hampshire Grants." Remarkably, slavery was outlawed in the republic.

In August 1777, Allen, while in custody in New York, learned of the death of his young son Joseph due to smallpox. In May 1778, he was exchanged for Colonel Archibald Campbell and reported to George Washington at Valley Forge. He would see no further action in the war.

Allen spent the next several years involved in Vermont's political and military matters and served as commander of the state's militia with the rank of Major General. During this time, some in Vermont negoitated a unification with Quebec, which was agreeable to the British, but following the surrender at Yorktown, Vermont sided with the Americans.

Statue of Ethan Allen at Fort Ticonderoga

On February 16, 1784, Allen married Frances "Fanny" Montresor Brush Buchanan after a brief courtship, and they had three children. That same year, Allen recovered the Deist manuscript from the estate of Thomas Young and had it published as *Reason- The Only Oracle of Man*. It is considered the first work published in the United States that openly attacked Christianity. The book was a financial and critical failure and undermined Allen's reputation as an iconic American Patriot.

On February 12, 1789, Allen died at his home in Burlington after suffering an apoplectic fit. He was buried in Green Mountain Cemetery in Burlington. The exact location of his remains within the cemetery is unknown. The magnificent columnar monument marking his grave may or may not actually be over his remains. Attempts have been made to settle the issue, including subsurface radar scans to detect remains, but the scans have remained inconclusive. The uncertainty has fueled an ongoing local controversy over the true burial site.

Vermont finally achieved statehood in 1791, after Allen's death.

Grave of Ethan Allen

Dr. Josiah Bartlett
(1729 – 1795)

First Vote for Independence

Buried at Plains Cemetery,
Kingston, New Hampshire.

**Continental Congress • Signer of the Declaration of Independence
Signer of the Articles of Confederation**

The first to vote for independence from Great Britain was the delegate from New Hampshire, who was also a physician. Dr. Josiah Bartlett said "Aye," and was then the second to sign the document after President John Hancock. Bartlett later signed the Articles of Confederation and served as Chief Justice of the New Hampshire Supreme Court. He was the first popularly elected governor of the state.

Josiah Bartlett was born on November 21, 1729, in Amesbury, Massachusetts, the fifth child and fourth son of Deacon Stephen Bartlett, a shoemaker, and his wife Hannah (née Webster) Bartlett. Stephen was the son of Richard and Hannah (Emery) Bartlett, and according to one genealogical study, the Bartlett line can be traced back to John Bartlett, Sr., who came to Newbury, Massachusetts, in 1634, on the ship *Mary and John*. Josiah's maternal grandfather was said to be "wealthy in landed property."

Young Josiah study Latin and Greek in his teens but likely due to the family's circumstances, received a limited education. Soon, he was apprenticed to a relative, Dr. Nehemiah Ordway, with whom he studied

Dr. Josiah Bartlett

medicine. At just twenty years of age, in 1750, and after three years of studies, Josiah moved to Kingston, New Hampshire, and started medical practice. At the time, Kingston was a frontier community where his services were greatly needed, being the only doctor in the county. With the proceeds, in 1751, he purchased land and a farm.

Josiah married his first cousin, Mary Barton Bartlett (1730-1789), the daughter of his uncle Joseph and his wife, Sarah (née Hoyt) Bartlett, on January 15, 1754. Mary was from nearby Newton, New Hampshire. Together, the Bartletts had eleven children: Mary (1754), Lois (1756), Miriam (1758), Rhoda (1760), Hannah (1762, did not survive), Levi (1753), Josiah (1765, did not survive), Josiah (1768), Ezra (1770), Sarah (1773), and Hannah (1776, did not survive). Three sons and five grandsons later became physicians.

In years past, the Kingston area was the center of an epidemic of "throat distemper," serious for adults and often fatal for young children. In 1754, the illness was back, and Bartlett experimented with therapies and drugs, discovering that Peruvian bark aided recovery, saving many.

Josiah Bartlett next became involved in politics. In March 1757, he was elected as a selectman for the town of Kingston, a position he held until 1775 when the town's government was dissolved by the royal governor at the outset of the Revolution.

In 1763, Bartlett was behind several real estate ventures, settling the town of Warren, New Hampshire, where Bartlett was the original grantee. He served in the same capacity for the villages of Wentworth and Sudbury, and was the proprieter for Salisbury and Perrystown (now Sutton).

In 1765, Bartlett was elected to the colonial assembly and joined in a three-year partnership for a medical practice with Dr. Amos Gale in Kingston.

In 1767, Bartlett became the colonel of the county militia, was appointed justice of the peace by Governor John Wentworth, and was asked to propose reforms to provincial laws.

The governor and Bartlett continued their close collaboration in 1770 when Wentworth asked Bartlett to help establish a system of equitable taxation for the colony. Following the Boston Massacre in March 1770, Bartlett was commissioned a lieutenant in the 7th New Hampshire Regiment in November.

By 1774, the friendship with Governor Wentworth was greatly strained. That year, in response to the Intolerable Acts following the Boston Tea Party, Bartlett was appointed to a committee of correspondence and attended the First Provincial Congress, held in Exeter, New Hampshire, after Wentworth dissolved the colonial assembly. This body sent delegates to the new Continental Congress in Philadelphia.

As tensions mounted later that year, the Bartlett home was destroyed by fire, allegedly set by Tories. After moving his family to their farmhouse, he commenced on reconstruction. Bartlett was selected as a delegate to the Continental Congress but declined so he could attend to his family and home. While still in New Hampshire, Bartlett alerted the state militia about a raid on British arms and gunpowder at Fort William and Mary in Portsmouth Harbor on December 14 and 15, 1774. Bartlett helped prepare for the British response. Angered at Bartlett's behavior and attendance at the Second Provincial Congress in January 1775, Governor Wentworth revoked Bartlett's various positions prior to being expelled.

Bartlett was elected to the Third Provincial Congress in the Spring of 1775 and wrote letters of support to Massachusetts following the clashes at Lexington and Concord. On August 23, 1775, Bartlett was elected as a delegate to the Second Continental Congress, and through early 1776, was the only representative from New Hampshire in Philadelphia, forcing him to participate on all of the committees. Bartlett wrote often to his wife. In one of the letters, he worried about potential outcomes, but left the results to higher powers:

> Kind Providence will order all things for the best, and if Sometimes affairs turn out Contrary to our wishes, we must make our selves Easy & Contented, as we are not Certain what is for the best.

During the second session, Bartlett was joined by delegates William Whipple and Matthew Thornton. On July 1, 1776, when the draft of the Declaration of Independence was circulating, Bartlett wrote to John Langdon, then the President of New Hampshire:

> The affair of Independency has been this day determined in a Committee of the whole House; by next Post, I expect you will receive a formal declaration with the reasons; the Declaration before Congress is, I think, a pretty good one. I hope it will not be spoiled by canvassing in Congress.

When the question of declaring independence from Britain was proposed, the vote was processed from the northernmost colony to the southernmost. Thus, New Hampshire was called first, and Bartlett the first delegate. He voted in the affirmative and became the first to vote for independence.

During the remainder of July 1776, Bartlett was very interested in what form the new government would take. He shared with John Langdon the arrival of the constitutions of Virginia and New Jersey, which he suggested would be good models for New Hampshire.

On August 2, 1776, when many of the delegates signed the Declaration of Independence, Bartlett was the second to sign, following John Hancock, the President of Congress. Bartlett returned to New Hampshire in December 1776 and declined another term in Congress. Instead, he joined the militia as a doctor under General John Stark. At the Battle of Bennington in August 1777, he cared for wounded soldiers.

In 1778, Bartlett was named to a legislative committee in New Hampshire to consider the adoption of the Articles of Confederation.

Bartlett reluctantly agreed to again join the Continental Congress in Philadelphia, where he signed the Articles of Confederation on behalf of New Hampshire and then returned home.

In 1779, Bartlett served as a judge on the Court of Common Pleas and as a member of the State Executive Council. Bartlett was elected to the New Hampshire State Legislature and named a delegate to the state's constitutional convention.

Despite not being a lawyer, Bartlett was appointed a justice on the State Superior Court in 1781. In 1782, he was appointed to the New Hampshire Supreme Court. In 1784, he presided over the inaugural session of the new state legislature. In 1788, Bartlett was named Chief Justice of the New Hampshire Supreme Court and was a delegate, and part-time chairman, of the state's convention to adopt the U.S. Constitution. Bartlett supported ratification, which occurred June 21, 1788. The legislature then named Bartlett as one of the state's first Senators, but Bartlett declined, his wife had failing health and passed away on July 14, 1789.

In 1790, Bartlett was selected as the Chief Executive of New Hampshire ("governor") under the new state constitution. He was re-elected three times. In 1792, he was the state's first popularly elected governor. He started the New Hampshire Medical Society, and upon his retirement as governor, became the society's first president.

Less than a year after his final term as governor, Bartlett suffered a stroke on May 19, 1795, and died in Kingston at age 65. He was buried next to his wife in the family sarcophagus at the Congregationalist Church in Kingston (now Plains Cemetery).

Bartlett's son of the same name (1768–1838) served in the US House of Representatives in the Twelfth Congress (1811–1813). A distant relative, Roscoe Gardner Bartlett also served as a Congressman more recently (1993–2013).

The town of Bartlett, New Hampshire, is named after Josiah. Relatives still live in the home at 156 Main Street in Kingston, now a historic landmark. A bronze statue of Bartlett stands in the town square in Amesbury, Massachusetts, and his portrait hands in the New Hampshire State House in Concord. It was drawn from the original by John Trumbull. Bartlett's name dons an elementary school, and he is the subject of a historical marker on New Hampshire Route 111 in Kingston. The Bartlett School operated in Amesbury, Massachusetts, and is now known as the Bartlett Museum, a nonprofit corporation.

The main character in the NBC drama series *The West Wing* was President Josiah Bartlet. Though a fictional character with a slightly different spelling, this Josiah played by Martin Sheen claimed lineage to the signer of the Declaration of Independence.

Grave of Dr. Josiah Bartlett

Nathaniel Folsom
(1726 – 1790)

Merchant Militiaman

Buried at Winter Street Cemetery,
Exeter, New Hampshire.

Continental Association

Nathaniel Folsom was a delegate to the Continental Congress from New Hampshire and the Major General of the New Hampshire Militia. He was also a merchant and holder of several state offices. Folsom signed the Continental Association as a member of the First Continental Congress in 1774.

Nathaniel Folsom was born in Exeter, Rockingham County, New Hampshire, on September 18, 1726, the son of Jonathan Folsom and his wife, Ann (née Ladd) Folsom. Nathaniel was the eighth of twelve children, including siblings Anna, Sarah, Lydia, Elizabeth, Abigail, John, Mary, Jonathan, Samuel, Josiah, and Trueworthy. His ancestors were early settlers in Massachusetts and were related to the Gilmans.

Young Nathaniel attended public schools. When his father died in 1740, when he was thirteen, he took employment with a merchant. As a young man, he invested in timber and opened a sawmill. He married first Dorothy Smith (1726–1776), with whom he had seven children: Nathaniel, Dorothy, Jonathan, Anna, Arthur, Mary, and Deborah. Both Deborah and Mary later married John Taylor Gilman, the Governor of

An imagined Nathaniel Folsom.

New Hampshire. Nathaniel married second Mary Sprague, with whom he had a daughter Ruth.

With the outbreak of the French and Indian War in 1754, Folsom joined the militia. The next year, he was a captain in Colonel Joseph Blanchard's New Hampshire Provincial Regiment under Sir William Johnson during the Crown Point expedition. At the Battle of Lake George, his company captured the French commander-in-chief, Major General Jean-Armand Baron de Dieskau, the baggage train, and critical supplies. Only six men were lost in his company. Over the rest of the war, Folsom was promoted to major, lieutenant colonel, and then colonel of the Fourth Regiment of the New Hampshire militia.

In 1761, Folsom partnered with his cousins, Joseph and Josiah Gilman, to form the merchant company Folsom, Gilman & Gilman. They operated a general store, a shipbuilding operation, and imported and exported goods. Folsom split from his cousins in 1768 but continued in the timber, lumber, and trade industries. He also became involved in local politics in Exeter, moderating town meetings.

Folsom was a delegate in July 1774, when the revolutionary assembly was convened. They sent him as a delegate to the First Continental

Congress in Philadelphia. He attended sessions from September 5, 1774, the Continental Congress's first day, through October 26, 1774. The Continental Association, limiting imports and exports to and from England, was adopted on October 20. Folsom was a signatory.

With the increase in hostilities, Governor Wentworth revoked Folsom's commission as colonel of the militia. This did not deter Folsom from leading his troops to aid in protecting Boston during the British siege. His men safely escorted captured cannons from Portsmouth to Durham. Folsom was given the rank of major general of the New Hampshire militia, numbering about 2000 men. He sent some of his men to aid Fort Ticonderoga.

On April 1, 1777, Folsom was again elected to the Continental Congress. He arrived in Philadelphia on July 20 and began serving the following day. On September 18, word came of the pending invasion of Philadelphia by the British. Whether in haste or as his custom, Folsom hopped on a horse without a saddle and headed out to York. There, he participated in the debates concerning the Articles of Confederation and was against taxation methods being proposed. He felt it unfair to tax property but to exclude slaves in the calculations, as the southern delegates argued. Folsom voted against the Articles of Confederation.

He wrote,

> Inclosed, I send you a copy of the Articles of confederation [sic] as far as agreed to by Congress. The 9th article is, 'That the proportion of public expense incurred by the United States for their common defense and general welfare, to be paid by each State into the Treasury, be ascertained by the value of all lands within each state granted to or surveyed for any person, as such land and the buildings and improvements thereon, shall be estimated according to such mode as Congress shall from time to time direct.' This article was opposed by all the New England Delegates and we are yet in hopes of having it re-considered.

Folsom was a member of a delegation of congressmen who visited Valley Forge during the winter of 1777/78. He and the others reported on the terrible conditions to Congress. After his term ended, he returned to New Hampshire, where he was elected Executive Councilor in 1778. This role was essentially the co-governor of New Hampshire.

In 1783, Folsom was a delegate to New Hampshire's constitutional convention, serving as its president. He was then the chief justice on the Court of Common Pleas in Exeter. Folsom died at Exeter on May 26, 1790, and was buried at the Winter Street Cemetery.

Nathaniel Folsom's grave marker.

Nicholas Gilman
(1755 – 1814)

Soldier and Congressman

Buried at Exeter Cemetery,
Exeter, New Hampshire.

———•◆•———

U.S. Constitution • Military

On July 15, 2018, the authors traveled to Exeter, New Hampshire to attend the monument dedication ceremony honoring a Founder organized by his descendants. This patriot made a name for himself at the young age of 21 in his service in the Continental Army. After the Revolution, he represented New Hampshire in the Continental Congress. He was a delegate to the Constitutional Convention and the youngest signer of the document produced by that gathering. He later represented his state in both the House of Representatives and the United States Senate. A true soldier-statesman, his name was Nicholas Gilman.

———•◆•———

Gilman was born on August 3, 1755, in Exeter, New Hampshire. He was named after his father who was a shipbuilder and a politician. As a boy, he attended local public schools though it appears his education was limited. He went to work as a clerk in his father's trading house while his older brother John worked in the family's shipbuilding business. The taxes the English imposed on the colonies adversely affected these businesses. Soon after the shooting started at Lexington and Concord, Gilman volunteered to serve in the New Hampshire regiment of the

Portrait of Nicholas Gilman etched by Albert Rosenthal,
1888, based on a miniature in possession of the family.

Continental Army, serving in the 3rd New Hampshire Regiment under its commander Colonel Alexander Scammell.

In 1777 British forces under the command of General John Burgoyne were advancing from Canada and heading to New York. Gilman's regiment marched to Fort Ticonderoga to join other American forces in halting the British invasion. Burgoyne's experienced regulars proved too much for the American forces and Gilman with his regiment was forced to retreat to avoid capture. It was during this retreat that the American forces utilized delaying tactics to slow the British advance. Meanwhile, Gilman busied himself with the task of supervising the training of the men in his regiment. He and his men participated in two important battles at Freeman's Farm where they inflicted significant damage on the British forces. Though the Americans failed to drive Burgoyne's army from the field of battle, the English lost twice as many men. Eventually, Burgoyne was forced to surrender to the American forces under General Horatio Gates at Saratoga.

After the battle, Scammel led his troops to Philadelphia to reinforce the forces serving under General Washington. Gilman and his unit endured the harsh winter at Valley Forge. Washington selected Colonel Scammell to serve as the Continental Army's Adjutant General and Scammell made Gilman his assistant. In 1778 Gilman was promoted to the rank of captain. Gilman would see action with Washington's army for the remainder of the revolution including the decisive Battle of Yorktown. In the latter part of 1783, Gilman's father passed away and he retired from the army to return home to Exeter to run the family business.

In 1786 the New Hampshire legislature appointed Gilman to serve in the Continental Congress. This appointment, as well as his selection to represent his state at the Annapolis Convention, demonstrated that Gilman's history of service and organizational skills had made him a

New Hampshire Senator Maggie Hassan speaking at the dedication of the new grave marker for Nicholas Gilman at Exeter Cemetery in Exeter, New Hampshire on July 15, 2018 (photo by Lawrence Knorr).

Saluting the new grave stone after placing a new Sons of the
American Revolution marker (photo by Lawrence Knorr).

national leader. As such he was committed to changing the Articles of
Confederation which had proven to be ineffective in bringing the states
together as a nation.

In 1787 Gilman represented New Hampshire at the Constitutional
Convention in Philadelphia. Coming from one of the smaller states, he
championed compromises that gave those states equal representation in
the United States Senate with the larger states in the union. After signing
the Constitution produced by the Philadelphia Convention, he worked
with his brother John to ensure that New Hampshire ratified the government proposed in the document. It is not overstating the facts to say that
the influence of the Gilman brothers was a key to the ratification of the
Constitution in the Granite State by the narrow vote of 57-47.

Gilman's public service was far from at an end. In 1789 when the first
Congress of the United States met in New York, Gilman was there as a
member of the House of Representatives. He would serve as a member

of Congress for four terms. It was during this period that Gilman demonstrated his capacity for growth and change. He had been a Federalist in supporting the establishment of the stronger federal government that the Constitution provided. With that battle won, he became concerned with the necessity of protecting the common man from potential abuses of the government. He increasingly began siding with the Democratic-Republican party that was headed by Thomas Jefferson. When Jefferson was elected president, he appointed Gilman to the position of a federal bankruptcy commissioner.

In 1804 Gilman was elected to the United States Senate. As a senator, he voted against war with Britain in 1812. In 1814 he was returning home to New Hampshire during a Senate recess when he passed away in Philadelphia. He served his country until the day he took his last breath.

Gilman should be remembered for his belief in and strong support for a strong national government. Indeed he believed such a government

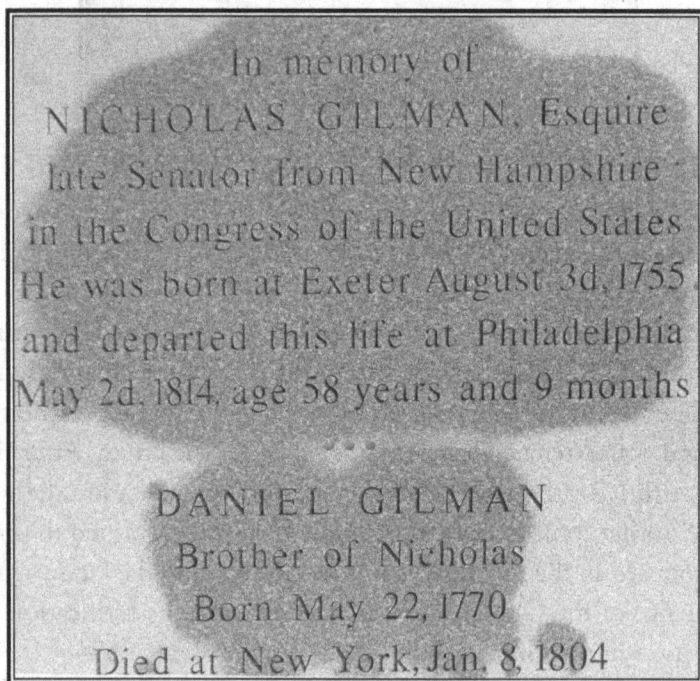

In memory of
NICHOLAS GILMAN, Esquire
late Senator from New Hampshire
in the Congress of the United States
He was born at Exeter August 3d, 1755
and departed this life at Philadelphia
May 2d, 1814, age 58 years and 9 months

DANIEL GILMAN
Brother of Nicholas
Born May 22, 1770
Died at New York, Jan. 8, 1804

Detail from Nicholas Gilman's new stone at Exeter Cemetery in Exeter,
New Hampshire (photo by Lawrence Knorr).

was necessary for the nation to survive. On the day after he signed the Constitution, he said that its adoption or rejection would determine "whether we shall become a respectable nation, or a people torn to pieces . . . and rendered contemptible for ages."

As mentioned previously, the authors attended the monument dedication ceremony honoring Nicholas Gilman held in July of 2018. The ceremony was both moving and appropriate. The guest speakers included two of Gilman's descendants, Mark Gilman and Quentin Gilman. One of Gilman's successors in the United States Senate, Maggie Hassan, also offered comments on Gilman's contributions as a Founding Father. The ceremony could easily serve as a model for honoring other Founders whose contributions have been ignored or forgotten for far too long.

John Langdon
(1741–1819)

Senator from New Hampshire

Buried at Old North Cemetery,
Portsmouth, New Hampshire.

United States Constitution

John Langdon was a revolutionary leader and one of the first two senators from New Hampshire. He was a successful international trader and owner of merchant vessels and contributed his business acumen and fortune to the independence movement. He served in the militia, the state legislature, the Continental Congress, as governor, US Senator, and as a delegate to the Constitutional Convention, where he signed the historic document. He was the first President Pro Tempore of the United States Senate.

John Langdon was born on his parents' farm in Portsmouth, New Hampshire, on June 26, 1741. He attended Major Samuel Hale's Latin School in Portsmouth and then worked as a clerk in Daniel Rindge's counting-house. Both Langdon and his older brother Woodbury rejected the opportunity to join their father's successful agricultural pursuits, succumbing instead to the lure of the sea. With the idea of entering the sea trade, they apprenticed themselves to local naval merchants. Through Rindge's business, John Langdon went on several voyages to the West Indies. By the age of 22, he was captain of a cargo ship, and within a few years, he would purchase his own ships, and soon he and his brother's company were taking such products as lumber and beef to various ports

John Langdon (1741–1819)

John Langdon

and returning with rum and sugar. By 1770 both men were rich and owned considerable property in the Portsmouth area.

The harsh economic measures enacted by England against the colonies, the seizure of a ship, *The Resolution*, which contained property of his, and the general atmosphere of interference in colonists' lives turned Langdon from apolitical to sympathizing with those who desired revolt against British rule. He served on the town committees elected to protest the tax Parliament enacted on the tea trade and to enforce a boycott of British goods organized throughout the colonies. In 1774 he was elected to the New Hampshire legislature, but growing impatient with politics, joined with a group of militiamen who raided Fort William and Mary (later renamed Fort Constitution) to seize munitions for use by the rebels.

On January 25, 1775, Langdon was elected to a seat in the Second Continental Congress. He immediately aligned himself with those calling for independence. He made significant contributions in his one year in congress by serving on the committee that oversaw the establishment of the Continental Navy. He resigned in June 1776 to become an agent to oversee prize ships—those taken or captured in war—and to supervise the construction of several warships, including the *Ranger,* which was captained by John Paul Jones, and the navy's first major warship the 74-gun *America.* Another of his responsibilities as a marine agent was supervising the importation and distribution of arms shipped from France to New England ports. These vital weapons were disguised in a complicated trade deal to maintain the appearance of French neutrality. The efforts to get cooperation and support from different states made Langdon feel strongly about a strong and efficient central government.

Elected again to the state legislature's lower house and rising to the rank of speaker, he devoted much of his energy to reorganizing the state militia into two brigades, one based in eastern New Hampshire and one in the west. Langdon himself took command of an elite company of light infantry in the Eastern brigade. Langdon's company of Light Horse Volunteers was often called a "silk stocking" outfit because it was composed of wealthy citizens selected from other units. Langdon financed the equipping of an expedition against British troops under British General John Burgoyne, and his company participated in the Battle of Bennington in August 1777. These troops played a major role in the victory and went on under General John Stark to force Burgoyne's surrender.

In 1778, Langdon's company participated in the Rhode Island campaign and was disbanded in the fall of that year. That ended Langdon's active military duty. Somehow amidst all this activity, he found time to get married to Elizabeth Sherburne, and the couple had one child, a daughter.

In 1784, he built at Portsmouth the mansion now known as the John Langdon House. Langdon was elected to two terms as President of New Hampshire, the title New Hampshire bestowed on its governor, one between 1785 and 1786 and then again between 1788 and 1789. In 1787 he was appointed to represent the state at the Constitutional Convention in Philadelphia. He was so anxious to attend that he paid his own expenses and that of fellow delegate Nicholas Gilman. At the convention, he soon became noted for his strong support of strengthening the national government. He signed the Constitution on September 17, 1787.

Langdon returned to New Hampshire and served as a delegate to the state convention that ratified the US Constitution. On June 21, 1788, New Hampshire's ratification was the ninth state to do so, putting the Constitution into effect. The vote was 57-47. He soon resigned as governor in 1789 to become one of the first US Senators. He served as the first president pro tempore and presided over the Senate's first session in which the electoral votes that made George Washington president were counted.

He retired from the Senate in 1801 and declined President Jefferson's offer to be Secretary of the Navy. Between then and 1812, he was active in New Hampshire politics. He was a member of the legislature from 1801 to 1805, twice holding the position of speaker. In 1805 he was elected governor and continued as such until 1811, except for a one-year hiatus in 1809. In 1812, due to his age and health, he refused the Democratic-Republican vice-presidential nomination to run with James Madison. He chose instead to retire from public office.

John Langdon died in Portsmouth on September 18, 1819, at 78. He was interred at the Old North Cemetery in Portsmouth. Langdon, New Hampshire, is named after him, as is Langdon Street in Madison, Wisconsin.

The tomb of John Langdon.

John Stark
(1728 – 1822)

"Hero of Bennington"

Buried at Stark Cemetery,
Manchester, New Hampshire.

———————

Military Commander

John Stark was a tough guy, a true warrior. He possessed an incredible ability to lead men in battle and a fierce independence and stubbornness that served him well during the French and Indian War and the Revolutionary War. He became known as the "Hero of Bennington" for his service at the Battle of Bennington in 1777.

———————

He was born in Londonderry, New Hampshire, on August 28, 1728. His father, Archibald, was born in Scotland and met his mother, Elizabeth, when he moved to Ireland. They emigrated from Ireland in 1720 and settled in Nutfield, New Hampshire. When Stark was eight years old, the family moved to Manchester, New Hampshire, formerly known as Derryfield. The couple had children who died during passage from Ireland and had six children born here.

The family home was destroyed by fire, and John and his brothers grew up on the wilderness frontier, becoming active hunters and trappers. They were accustomed to staying in forest camps, becoming inured to hardships and learning lessons of self-dependence. They had frequent contact with Indians from whom they obtained knowledge of their language and customs, and as a result, they became excellent marksmen.

John Stark (1728–1822)

John Stark

On April 28, 1752, while on a hunting and trapping trip along the Baker River, Stark was captured by Abenaki warriors and taken to the village of St. Francis in Quebec. While a captive, Stark was treated well by the Abenaki, who adopted him into the tribe. They admired his spunk and defiance. In later years, John would comment that he "had experienced more genuine kindness from the savages of St. Francis than he ever knew prisoners of war to receive from more civilized nations." In July, John was sold for $103 to a Mr. Wheelwright of Boston, hired to purchase white captives of Native Americans. He safely returned to New Hampshire.

Stark married Elizabeth (Molly) Page on August 20, 1758. The couple had eleven children, the oldest of whom, Caleb, served with his father in the 1st New Hampshire Regiment at the Battles of Bunker Hill, Trenton, and Princeton. He rose to the rank of Major and served in the New Hampshire Senate.

During the French and Indian War, Stark served as a second Lieutenant and member of Rogers' Rangers, a bold troop of colonial militia under Captain Robert Rogers' command. He fought in the Battle of Lake George and Bloody Pond and many others but would not participate in Rogers' October 4, 1759 raid against the Abenaki at St. Francis out of respect for his Indian foster parents who lived there. At the end of the war, Stark retired as a captain and returned to Derryfield. His time with the Rangers taught him tactics that would serve him well in the revolution to come.

Stark was at his sawmill when he heard of the battles at Lexington and Concord. He immediately went home, gathered his belongings and set out on the road towards Medford, Massachusetts. According to historian Thomas Fleming, within six hours, he enlisted half his regiment. Once he arrived in Medford, just outside of Boston, the New Hampshire men gathered to select a leader. On April 23, Stark accepted a Colonelcy in the New Hampshire militia and was given command of the 1st New Hampshire Regiment. The regiment consisted of 800 men. Thomas Fleming writes that Stark's men were "the best troops in the amorphous American army. Stark's men were much more used to handling guns than the majority of the Grand American Army. They were also considerably tougher".

During the siege of Boston, Stark's regiment was assigned to the northern flank of the Charlestown peninsula. Stark anticipated his opponent's, British General William Howe, next move by building a breastwork along the beach to prevent being flanked by Howe's light infantry. Stark predicted correctly as about 350 light infantrymen charged Stark's regiment. The 1st New Hampshire laid waste to several waves of British attackers until the remaining British troops retreated, losing one-third of their force. The day's New Hampshire dead were buried in Salem Street Burying Grounds in Medford.

Soon after the Battle of Bunker Hill, Washington offered Stark a command in the Continental Army, and he accepted. He and his New Hampshire regiment agreed to join the Continental Army. They were sent to Canada as reinforcements in the spring of 1776. The invasion failed, and Stark and his men joined Washington's main army. He successfully commanded his men at the Battles of Trenton and Princeton, after which he was sent home to recruit more troops, as the regiment was now half its original size. He was successful in recruitment but discovered that Congress had overlooked him for a promotion to the rank of brigadier general. Feeling outraged and betrayed, he tendered his resignation. When other generals tried to talk him out of it, he replied that a new British threat would be coming from Canada, and he would be ready to face it from New Hampshire. Four months later, he was offered the position of Brigadier General of the New Hampshire Militia, which he accepted on the condition that he not be answerable to the Continental Army.

Stark was right; as soon as British General John Burgoyne, heading south from Canada, sent an expedition to capture American supplies at

John Stark statue in the US Capitol

Bennington, Vermont. Stark learned of the approaching British troops and assembled his men at Bennington on August 13, 1777. On the 16th, the battle began when Stark's men attacked the British at Walloomsac, New York, ten miles from Bennington. Stark claimed it was "the hottest engagement I have ever witnessed." Darkness brought the battle to a halt, and it ended in an American victory. Stark's action contributed to the surrender of Burgoyne's northern army on October 17, following the Battles of Saratoga, by raising American morale, preventing the British from obtaining supplies, and eliminating several hundred enemy soldiers. Stark lost 14 men killed and 42 wounded. The British had 374 professional soldiers, and only 9 men escaped. For this feat, Stark was promoted to brigadier general in the Continental Army.

Burgoyne's surrender is regarded as a pivotal turning point in the Revolutionary War, as it marked the first major defeat of a British general and convinced the French that the Americans were worthy of military aid.

In September 1780, Stark sat as a judge in the court-martial that found British Major John André guilty of spying and aiding in Benedict Arnold's conspiracy to surrender West Point to the British.

Stark remained active throughout the remainder of the Revolutionary War, and Congress recognized his service on September 30, 1783, when he was promoted to the rank of major general.

Once the war ended, Stark chose to retire entirely. He returned to his farm in Manchester, New Hampshire, where he remained tending to it until he became too ill to do so. In 1809, a group of "Bennington" veterans gathered to commemorate the battle. Stark was not well enough to travel, but he sent a letter to his comrades, which closed with "Live free or die: death is not the worst of evils." New Hampshire would later (1945) adopt "Live free or die" as the state's motto.

Stark died at home on May 8, 1822, at the age of 93. He was buried in Stark Park in Manchester. He is memorialized in many ways and places. There is a New Hampshire historical marker near his birthplace, as well as a stone marker at the actual homestead location. The Daughters of the American Revolution owns his childhood home, and it is a National Historic Landmark. There is a bronze statue of General Stark in front of the New Hampshire statehouse in Concord and another in front of the West Annex of Manchester's City Hall. Stark and the Battle of Bennington are commemorated with a 306-foot-tall Bennington Battle Monument and a statue of Stark in Bennington, Vermont. In 1894, the State of New Hampshire donated a statue of General Stark for the National Statuary Hall of the United States Capitol.

Stark's grave

John Sullivan
(1740 – 1795)

Irish General

Buried at Sullivan Family Cemetery,
Durham, New Hampshire.

———◆———

**Continental Congress • Continental Association
Major General • Governor**

———◆———

John Sullivan was an Irish American lawyer from New Hampshire who became a Continental Congressman, Major General, Governor of the Granite State, and Federal judge. He was a signer of the Continental Association and led several military engagements during the Revolution, including the Delaware Crossing and Sullivan's Expedition against the Iroquois, who were loyal to the British.

———◆———

Sullivan, born on February 17, 1740, in Somersworth, New Hampshire, was the third son of Irish settlers from the Beara Peninsula, County Cork, John Owen "Eoghan" O'Sullivan and his wife Margery (née Browne) O'Sullivan. His father was a schoolteacher, the son of minor gentry in the Irish penal colony, Philip O'Sullivan. Because they were Catholics, they were reduced to peasants, though retaining their property. Upon emigrating to Maine, then in Massachusetts, John became a Protestant. Sullivan's brother, James Sullivan, was later a governor of Massachusetts, and brother Benjamin served in the Royal Navy and died before the American Revolution. Another brother, Captain David Sullivan, was kidnapped by the British on February 14, 1781, and later died of disease.

John Sullivan (1740–1795)

John Sullivan

Sullivan received a limited education in New Hampshire but studied law under attorney Samuel Livermore from 1758 to 1760. Soon after his admission to the New Hampshire bar in 1760, he married Lydia Worcester. The couple had six children, four of whom survived infancy: Lydia, John, James, and George (who later served as a United States Representative from New Hampshire).

Sullivan first practiced law beginning in 1763 in Berwick, now in Maine, and then moved to Durham, New Hampshire in 1764. For the next eight years, he grew his practice and expanded into milling. He joined the St. John's Lodge of Freemasons in Portsmouth in 1767 and remained a member for the rest of his life, rising to be the first Grand Master of the Grand Lodge of New Hampshire.

In 1772, Sullivan was appointed as a major in the New Hampshire colonial militia by his friend, Governor John Wentworth. In 1773, his law practice included Alexander Scammell. As tensions rose with the British, Sullivan was at odds with the governor and supported the Patriots. On July 21, 1774, he was appointed the delegate from Durham to the first Provincial Congress of New Hampshire. This assembly then sent him and Nathaniel Folsom to the First Continental Congress, where they arrived in time for the first meeting on September 5, 1774. They both signed the Continental Association on October 20, 1774.

Amid the gunpowder controversies, upon his return, Sullivan led a raid to take cannon and muskets on December 15, 1774, near Portsmouth. In January 1775, the New Hampshire Congress sent Sullivan and John Langdon to the Second Continental Congress. They arrived in time to discuss the hostilities at Lexington and Concord and the formation of the Continental Army. George Washington was appointed Commander in Chief, and Sullivan was made a Brigadier General. He left Philadelphia on June 27, 1775, to join the new Continental Army at the Siege of Boston. According to local legend, his troops used the password "St. Patrick" until the British left.

Following Britain's evacuation of Boston in the spring of 1776, Washington sent Sullivan to Quebec to replace John Thomas, who had died from smallpox. Sullivan inherited a division stricken with illness and unable to take Trois-Rivières, instead falling back to Crown Point. Congress sought a scapegoat for the failed invasion and attempted to pin the defeat on Sullivan. However, he was exonerated and then promoted to Major General on August 9, 1776.

Sullivan next joined Washington at Long Island and was put in command of half of the defense in tandem with senior officer Israel Putnam on August 23, 1776. During the Battle of Long Island on August 27, there was confusion in command; Sullivan personally fought bravely against the Hessians at Battle Pass, pistols in each hand. To no avail, he was captured by the British.

While in captivity, the Howe brothers, General and Admiral, convinced Sullivan to attend a peace conference with the Congress. Sullivan was sent as a peace delegate and managed to have the meeting. John Adams, however, shut it down, referring to Sullivan as a "decoy duck." The peace conference failed, and Sullivan returned to captivity until exchanged for Lieutenant General Richard Prescott.

Sullivan returned to the army in time to help lead the attack on Trenton on December 26, 1776, which led to the capture of many Hessians. He then performed well at the Battle of Princeton. At Brandywine in September 1777, Sullivan's troops were surprised by the

British but left the field in an orderly manner, reinforced by Nathanael Greene. At Germantown, Sullivan's men were routing the British light infantry, but then heavy fog and delayed movements prevented victory and caused confusion, leading to friendly fire on his troops.

In early 1778, Sullivan led Continental troops and militia at Rhode Island, working together with the French Navy to capture Newport, which was held by the British. The French Admiral d'Estaing found his ships damaged and scattered in a storm, leaving Sullivan to himself. Sullivan's troops then fought a retreat in Rhode Island. Sullivan felt the French had dishonored him.

Next, in the summer of 1779, Sullivan led an expedition against the Iroquois in Pennsylvania and upstate New York. The Six Nations had been hostile to the colonists, raiding settlements. Sullivan and three thousand men gathered in northeastern Pennsylvania and marched towards Tioga in upstate New York, adding another one thousand men on the way.

At one point, Sullivan pushed his troops so hard that his horses became unusable and had to be killed. The spot where this occurred is known as Horseheads, New York. Due to Congress's tepid reaction and Sullivan's mounting financial issues back home, he retired from the military and returned to New Hampshire, where he was seen as a hero.

Sullivan was again elected to the Continental Congress by the legislature in November 1780, though it was against his wishes. Sullivan reluctantly returned to Congress and was immediately embroiled in dealing with the status of Vermont, whether it should be part of New York, New Hampshire, or independent. A possible alliance with the British in Canada also loomed, leading to Vermont becoming a separate state. Sullivan became embroiled in controversy when he borrowed money from the French minister to Congress that was likely not to be repaid. Sullivan, in turn, was accused of favoring the French in Congress, tarnishing his reputation. As the war came to an end, Sullivan was involved in deciding on peace negotiators who would favor the French, including Benjamin Franklin. One of his last acts was to vote Robert Livingston to the position of Secretary of Foreign Affairs over John Adams, who had been lobbying for it. He then resigned from Congress a month early, on August 11, 1781. Though historian George Bancroft, one hundred years later, declared that Sullivan had taken French bribes and shown them favor, there was no direct proof, and Sullivan was exonerated by other historians.

Back in New Hampshire, Sullivan was named New Hampshire's Attorney General, serving from 1782 until 1786. He was also elected to

John Sullivan memorial

General John Sullivan's house in Durham, New Hampshire.

the state assembly and served as its speaker. Sullivan was one of the 31 founding members of The Society of the Cincinnati in New Hampshire on November 18, 1783. He was elected the first President of the New Hampshire Society, serving until 1793.

He led the ratification of the US Constitution in New Hampshire on June 21, 1788. He was then President (now Governor) of New Hampshire in 1786 when he quelled the Exeter Rebellion, also known as the Paper Money Riot, in the midst of Shay's Rebellion by calling up over two thousand militia. He led the state again in 1787 and 1789.

Sullivan was appointed a US District Court Judge for New Hampshire by President Washington on September 24, 1789, and confirmed by the Senate on September 26. However, due to poor health, he was not seated until 1792.

Justice Sullivan died at home in Durham, New Hampshire, on January 23, 1795, and was interred in the family cemetery behind the house. Said his obituary in the *American Minerva*:

> The character of that hon. Gentleman is the part he took in his Country's interest, when great and patriotic exertions were necessary; His tried and distinguished abilities in various high, and

important offices; and his public and private virtues, are all well known to his Fellow-citizens of United America.

Counties in New Hampshire, Missouri, New York, Pennsylvania, and Tennessee are named for him. The towns of Sullivan in New Hampshire and New York are named after him. Bridges in New Hampshire and Pennsylvania carry his name, as does a street in Greenwich Village in Manhattan. The Sullivan Trail follows some of Sullivan's 1779 Expedition in northeast Pennsylvania and Sullivan Way in Trenton is named for him.

Sullivan's father outlived him, dying at 104 in June 1795. A statue honoring Sullivan was erected in 1894 in Durham. His house, known as The General John Sullivan House, is privately owned and occupied and is on the National Register of Historic Landmarks.

Grave of John Sullivan

Matthew Thornton
(1714–1803)

First Speaker of the New Hampshire Assembly

Buried at Thornton Family Burying Ground,
Merrimack, New Hampshire.

———•◦•———

Continental Congress • Declaration of Independence • Military

Matthew Thornton was a physician, judge, and member of the New Hampshire Provincial Congress. As a member of the Continental Congress from late 1776 until May 1777, he was a signer of the Declaration of Independence on behalf of New Hampshire. For a time, he was the Speaker of the New Hampshire House of Representatives.

———◆◦◆———

Thornton was born on March 3, 1714, in Lisburn, County Antrim, Ireland (now in Northern Ireland), the son of James Thornton and Elizabeth (née Jenkins) Thornton, poor Irish farmers near Belfast.

When Thornton was about three years old, the family emigrated to North America and settled first in Wiscasset, Massachusetts Bay Colony (now Maine). Following an Indian attack on July 11, 1722, the family fled their burning home and resettled in Worcester, Massachusetts.

Thorton was educated in the local schools of Worcester and then studied medicine under Dr. Grout. In approximately 1740, he completed these studies and moved to Londonderry, New Hampshire, to establish a medical practice.

Early in his career as a physician, Thornton served as a surgeon in the New Hampshire Militia in the successful expedition to capture Fortress

Matthew Thornton

Louisbourg on Cape Breton in 1745. Upon his return, he focused on building his medical practice and acquiring land.

From 1758 through 1762, Thornton served in the New Hampshire Provincial Assembly. During this period, in 1760, at age 46, he married eighteen-year-old Hannah Jack. The couple ultimately had five children.

On July 6, 1763, Thornton was granted a township in his name by Benning Wentworth, then the Governor of New Hampshire. However, in 1765, with the announcement of the Stamp Act, Thornton voiced his opinion against it. Regardless, Governor Wentworth still named Thornton a colonel in the militia. By 1771, Thornton was also a justice of the peace for the County of Hillsborough, New Hampshire.

As the Revolutionary War commenced in 1775, Thornton sided with the rebels, denouncing the royal government in New Hampshire. Thornton was then appointed the President of the Provincial Congress, which met on June 14, 1775, to fill the vacuum left by the flight of Governor Wentworth. Said Thornton, now the presiding officer of the whole state, to the Congress:

Friends and brethren, you must all be sensible that the affairs of America have, at length, come to a very affecting and alarming crisis. The horrors and Distresses of a Civil War, which, till of late, we only had in contemplation, we now find ourselves obliged to realize. Painful, beyond expression, have been those Scenes of blood and devastation, which the barbarous cruelty of British troops have placed before our eyes. Duty to God—to ourselves—to Posterity—enforced by the cries of slaughtered Innocents, have urged us to take up arms in our own defence. Such a day as this, was never before known, either to us or to our Fathers. You will give u leave, therefore, in whom you have reposed special confidence as your representative body, to suggest a few things, which call for the serious attention of every northeast, who has the true interest of America at Heart. We would therefore recommend to the colony at large to cultivate that christian [sic] Union, Harmony and tender affection, which is the only foundation upon which our invaluable privileges can rest, with any security; or our publick measures be pursued with the least prospect of success . . . We seriously and earnestly recommend the practice of that pure and undefiled religion, which embalmed the memory of our pious ancestors, as that alone upon which we can build a solid hope and confidence in the Divine protection and favour, without whose blessing all the measures of safety we have, or can propose, will end in our shame and disappointment.

That November, at the second Provincial Congress, Thornton was renewed as a colonel in the militia, a position he held until November 1779. He also oversaw the drafting of the first state constitution for New Hampshire, which was adopted on January 5, 1776, the first for any rebelling colony. The delegates then elected Thornton as the first Speaker of the New Hampshire Assembly.

Thornton was elected to an open seat in the Continental Congress on September 12, 1776. He arrived in Philadelphia on November 4, 1776, four months after the Declaration of Independence was passed. On that date, he became the third person from New Hampshire to sign the document, following Josiah Bartlett and William Whipple. Thornton was reelected to the Continental Congress on December 24, 1776, but only served until May 2, 1777.

John Adams, in a letter to his wife, Abigail, wrote of Thornton:

> We have from New Hampshire a Col. Thornton, a Physician by Profession, a Man of Humour. He has a large Budget of droll Stories, with which he entertains Company Perpetually. I heard about Twenty or five and twenty Years ago, a Story of a Physician in Londonderry, who accidentally [met] with one of our new England Enthusiasts, call'd [Exhorters]. The Fanatic soon began to examine the Dr. [concerning] the Articles of his Faith, and what he thought of original Sin? Why, says the Dr., I satisfy myself about it in this manner. Either original Sin is divisible or indivisible. If it was divisible every descendant of Adam and Eve must have a Part, and the share which falls to each Individual at this Day, is so small a Particle, that I think it is not worth considering. If indivisible, then the whole Quantity must have descended in a right Line, and must now be possessed by one Person only, and the Chances are Millions and Millions to one that that Person is now in Asia or Africa, and that I have nothing to do with it. I told Thornton the story and that I suspected him to be the Man. He said he was. He belongs to Londonderry.

Thornton should not be confused with his namesake nephew. Captain Matthew Thornton was charged with treason before the Battle of Bennington in 1777. Daniel Webster's father, Ebenezer Webster, investigated the allegations. Thornton was found not guilty and was discharged.

Following his service in the Continental Congress, Thornton, now in his sixties, served as a judge on the New Hampshire Superior Court until 1782. During this time, he wrote political essays and retired from his medical practice to Merrimack, New Hampshire. There, he operated a farm and a ferry with his family.

In his later years, Thornton remained involved in politics. He served as the representative of Merrimack and Bedford in the New Hampshire House of Representatives in 1783, and in the New Hampshire Senate from 1784 to 1787, while also serving as a state counselor from 1785 to 1786, and again as the representative for Merrimack in 1786.

Sadly, his wife Hannah, 28 years his junior, died in 1786, perhaps signaling the end of his public life.

While visiting his daughter in Newburyport, Massachusetts, Thornton died on June 24, 1803, at age 89. *The Farmer's Cabinet* stated:

> His Character needs not the aid of a newspaper panegyric: His life is its best eulogium. It exhibited at once the Christian and the Patriot, and was a proof that he united the love of God with the love of his country. He engaged early in the cause of American

Grave of Matthew Thornton

Independence, and continued to his death a firm friend to the constitution and government of his country. His private virtues were a model for imitation, and, while memory does her office, will be had in grateful recollection.

Thornton was buried next to his wife at the Thornton Family Burying Ground in Merrimack, New Hampshire.

Thornton is honored in several ways, including the naming of a town and an elementary school after him. His former home is on the National Register of Historic Places, and a historical marker featuring him was erected on US Route 3 in Merrimack. In 1873, his great-grandson, US Navy Captain James S. Thornton of the *Kearsarge*, donated a portrait of Thornton to the state of New Hampshire.

John Wentworth Jr.
(1745 – 1787)

New Hampshire Scion

Buried at Pine Hill Cemetery,
Dover, New Hampshire.

Continental Congress • Articles of Confederation

John Wentworth Jr. was an attorney from a famous New Hampshire family. As a member of the Continental Congress from 1778 until 1779, he was a signer of the Articles of Confederation on behalf of New Hampshire.

Wentworth was born on July 17, 1745, near the Salmon Falls River at Somersworth, Strafford County, New Hampshire, the son of Judge John Wentworth and Joanna (née Gilman) Wentworth, a descendant of "Elder" William Wentworth who emigrated to America in the mid-1600s and had blood ties to King Edward VI of England and Sir Thomas Wentworth, the Earl of Strafford, for whom Strafford County, New Hampshire, was named. Two other John Wentworths were descendants of "Elder" including John Wentworth (1672-1730), a lieutenant governor of New Hampshire, and Sir John Wentworth (1737-1820), the last colonial governor of New Hampshire, and a first cousin once removed to the signer.

Wentworth was tutored privately and then entered Harvard College, where he graduated in 1768. He then began studying law in Dover, New

York Courthouse where the Continental Congress approved the
Articles of Confederation.

Hampshire. He was admitted to the New Hampshire bar in 1771, but
did not open a law practice. Instead, Governor John Wentworth appointed him as the register of probate for Strafford County from 1773
until his death.

On January 1, 1774, siding with the revolutionaries, Wentworth
was named to the New Hampshire Committee of Correspondence
against the wishes of his family. This put him at odds with the governor
and other Loyalist family members. It was the various Committees of
Correspondence that agreed to call for a Continental Congress.

On May 11, 1775, the New Hampshire Provincial Congress held
a Convention of Deputies at Exeter, New Hampshire, of which young
Wentworth, not yet thirty, was the chair. This committee elected John
Langdon and John Sullivan to the First Continental Congress.

From 1776 through 1780, Wentworth, representing Dover, was
elected to the New Hampshire House of Representatives, which succeed-
ed the colonial government during the Revolution. In 1777, Wentworth
was also named to the New Hampshire Committee of Safety.

On March 14, 1778, Wentworth was elected to the Continental
Congress, still meeting in York, Pennsylvania, after the authoring of the

Articles of Confederation. Wentworth attended the Congress from May 30 to June 18, 1778, and then affixed his signature on behalf of New Hampshire on July 9, 1778. A letter from Josiah Bartlett, New Hampshire Congressman, to Meshech Weare, the President of New Hampshire, on July 11, 1778, stated, "Mr. Wentworth had a fever at York Town; it was pretty bad. I tarried with him for four days after the Congress adjourned; left him better Thursday the 2nd instant; have not heard from him since; hope he will be here the beginning of the week."

Grave of John Wentworth Jr.

On August 18, 1778, Bartlett wrote to William Whipple, "Mr. Wentworth is in town but does not attend public business." However, Wentworth was reelected to Congress the next day on August 19, 1778.

The following month, on September 8, 1778, Bartlett again wrote to Weare: "I have Reced [received] a Copy of the appointment of Delegates to attend Congress the first of November next, and I must beg leave inform you That I can by no means attend Congress after the last of october [sic] next. By reason of Mr. Wentworth's Sickness I have not Recd. the least assistance from him, and am obliged to attend so Closely to public business without any interval of Relaxation, that it will be necessary for my Constitution of body and mind to be relieved then, if I am able to hold out till that time."

It appears that Wentworth did not attend the Congress again. On April 3, 1779, Nathaniel Peabody and Woodbury Langdon were elected to the Congress in place of Bartlett and Wentworth, who had resigned. Rather, Wentworth remained in the New Hampshire House of Representatives. In 1781, he replaced his father as a member of the state executive council, in support of Meshech Weare. He was also a member of the New Hampshire Committee of Safety.

In 1783, Wentworth was elected to the New Hampshire Senate and left the executive council. He served through 1786.

Wentworth died at age 41 on January 10, 1787, at Dover, New Hampshire. He was interred at Pine Hill Cemetery in Dover.

William Whipple
(1730–1785)

Hero of Saratoga

Buried at Old North Cemetery,
Portsmouth, New Hampshire.

Continental Congress • Declaration of Independence • Military

---

William Whipple was a merchant and ship's captain who later became
a judge. As a member of the Continental Congress from 1776 to 1779,
he was a signer of the Declaration of Independence on behalf of New
Hampshire. As a soldier, he commanded brigades in the New Hampshire
Militia at Saratoga and during the Battle of Rhode Island.

Whipple was born on January 14, 1730, in Kittery, Massachusetts
(now in Maine), the son of Captain William Whipple, Sr., and Mary
(née Cutt) Whipple, the daughter of a wealthy shipbuilder. Some sources
described Whipple Sr. as a brewer or "maltster." Regardless, they were an
old Massachusetts Bay Colony family, descended from Samuel Appleton.

Master Whipple attended the common schools in Kittery and then
went to sea. By age 21, he was a ship's master. Soon, he purchased his
own ship and traded in commodities, engaging in the triangular trade
between North America, Africa, and the West Indies, dealing in wood,
rum, and slaves.

Circa 1759, Whipple went into business with his brother Joseph in
Portsmouth and dropped the slave trade. He also later freed any slaves in
his household, including a servant named Prince Whipple, and refused

William Whipple

to deal with the issue further. Whipple hoped for the abolition of the slave trade throughout America.

In 1767, Whipple married his first cousin, Catherine Moffat. They moved into the Moffatt-Ladd House in Portsmouth in 1769, but their only child, a son name William III, died as an infant.

Early in 1775, as the rebellion against the crown was starting, the people of New Hampshire elected a Provincial Congress. On February 6, 1775, it was reported that John Wentworth, Nathaniel Folsom, Meshech Weare, Josiah Bartlett, Christopher Toppan, Ebenezer Thompson, and William Whipple were elected to the committee. Whipple was also appointed to the Committee of Safety for New Hampshire and was elected to the Continental Congress along with Josiah Bartlett and John Langdon.

Prior to leaving for the Continental Congress, Whipple wrote to fellow Congressman Josiah Bartlett, anticipating the work ahead: "This year, my Friend, is big with mighty events. Nothing less than the fate of America depends on the virtue of her sons, and if they do not have virtue enough to support the most Glorious Cause ever human beings were engaged in, they don't deserve the blessings of freedom."

Whipple arrived at the Continental Congress in Philadelphia on February 29, 1776. He served through September 24, 1779. During the summer of 1776, Whipple and fellow New Hampshire delegates Josiah Bartlett and Matthew Thornton signed the Declaration of Independence. Whipple was also the second cousin of Stephen Hopkins, another signer from Rhode Island.

Early in 1777, with the war going poorly to the south, the New Hampshire Assembly established two brigades of militia for the defense of the state. Command of one was given to Whipple, and the other to John Stark. At this time, Whipple's servant, Prince Whipple, urged his master to allow him to also fight for the cause. "You are going to fight for liberty," he said, "but I have none to fight for." Whipple granted Prince's request to fight and emancipated Prince upon the conclusion of his military service.

Following service in the Continental Congress, during the summer of 1777, Whipple traveled back to New Hampshire with fellow Congressman William Ellery from Rhode Island. Whipple kept meticulous notes about his travels, which survive to this day.

The New Hampshire militia saw action that autumn at Saratoga in September and October. Whipple commanded four militia regiments, including Bellow's, Chase's, Moore's, and Welch's. Following the great victory, Major General Horatio Gates selected Whipple and Colonel James Wilkinson to negotiate the British surrender with two of their counterparts under General Burgoyne. Whipple was one of the signers of the Convention of Saratoga. Whipple then escorted Burgoyne and his army back to Winter Hill, Somerville, Massachusetts. He passed the news of the victory to Captain John Paul Jones, who later informed Benjamin Franklin in Paris.

The following year, during the Battle of Rhode Island, Whipple led three regiments under the command of General John Sullivan. This battle did not go as well, and when Sullivan ordered a retreat, Whipple and his men, who resided in a house near the battlefield, were within cannon shot of the advancing British. One cannonball tore through a horse out-side the house and smashed the leg of one Whipple's subordinates, later requiring amputation.

Returning to the Continental Congress in 1779, Whipple was not shy in his letters to his colleagues, complaining about the difficulties of being in the Congress, according to one source:

> "Discontent over pay and allowances frequently resulted in del-egates threatening to return home. As his ragged clothes fell off his back and his 'lady of the tub' badgered him over failure to pay for his freshly washed socks, [James] Lovell demanded 'ninety days of refreshment' from the Continental Congress. He admit-ted to Sam Adams that Congress, 'this political scene of drudgery,' had become too expensive for him to attend. In 1779, [John] Fell similarly observed that New Jersey's parsimony did not tempt him to stay in Congress 'longer than I had engaged for,' and William Whipple declared that 'there is no pecuniary temptation that will be a temptation to tarry through the summer.'"

That November, the Continental Congress appointed Whipple and Thomas Waring to the Board of Admiralty, but Whipple returned to New Hampshire and was elected to the New Hampshire Assembly in 1780, serving until 1784. During this time, he was elected one of the "Overseers of the Poor," and on October 11, 1782, he was one of the judges, along with David Brearly, William Churchill Houston, Cyrus Griffin, Joseph Jones, and Thomas Nelson, to help resolve the land dis-pute over the Wyoming Valley between Pennsylvania and Connecticut. The court was held in Trenton, New Jersey, on November 12, 1782. Also, in 1782, Whipple was appointed as a justice on the Supreme Court of New Hampshire, a position he held until his death.

It was while riding on his judicial circuit at only age 55 on November 28, 1785, that Justice Whipple suffered a cardiac episode and fainted, falling off his horse. Whipple died that day and was buried at the Old North Cemetery in Portsmouth, New Hampshire.

A Maryland newspaper declared him "a Gentleman of a very amiable Character."

Another newspaper in New Hampshire eulogized him: "On Monday, the 28th ultimo, died, universally lamented, the Hon. General William Whipple, a Judge of the Superior Court of this State. In him, concentrated every principle of the dignity of man. His disinterested patriotism and public services are now known to all; and when newspaper encomiums are lost in oblivion, the pen of the historian shall preserve the remembrance of his virtues in the breast of succeeding generations."

Whipple's original tombstone reads:

"Here are deposited the remains of the Honourable William Whipple, who departed this Life on the 28th day of November, 1785, in the 55th Year of his Age. He was often elected and thrice attended the Continental Congress, as Delegate for the State of New Hampshire, particularly in that memorable Year in which America declared itself independent of Great Britain. He was also at the Time of his decease a Judge of the Supreme Court of Judicature. In Him a firm and ardent Patriotism, was united with universal benevolence, and every social Virtue."

Grave of William Whipple

Paine Wingate
(1739–1838)

Last Continental Congressman to Die

Buried at Stratham Cemetery,
Stratham, New Hampshire.

***

Continental Congress • US Senate • US House of Representatives

Paine Wingate had a long life, much of it in public service. He was an American preacher, farmer, and statesman from New Hampshire. He served in the Continental Congress and both the United States Senate, where he was an inaugural member, and the United States House of Representatives.

***

He was born in Amesburg, Massachusetts, on May 14, 1739, the sixth of twelve children. His father, Paine Sr., was a minister in Amesburg. The young Paine graduated from Harvard in 1759 and became a minister, too. He was ordained as pastor of the Congregational Church in 1763. His pastorate was not successful and was full of controversy. He resigned in 1776 to become a farmer.

He married Eunice Pickering, the sister of Timothy Pickering, on May 23, 1765, in Essex, Massachusetts. Records show they had at least three sons and five daughters. He was held in high esteem by members of his community and in 1775 was appointed to represent his town at the Fourth Provincial Congress of New Hampshire. At that time, Wingate expressed the opinion that pacification with England was still possible.

He was elected to several terms in the New Hampshire House of Representatives and was a delegate to the state Constitutional Convention in 1781.

Paine Wingate

In 1788 he served in the Continental Congress and was a strong advocate of ratification of the United States Constitution writing, "Those who are well-wishers to their country, and best know the situation we are in, are most sensible of the necessity of its adoption, and great pains are taken to obtain the end."

New Hampshire appointed him to the first United States Senate, in which he served from March 4, 1789, until March 3, 1793. He was present when the first President, George Washington, took the oath of office. At that time, the Senate's business was conducted in secret. Wingate supported this saying, "How would all the little domestic transactions of even the best regulated family appear if exposed to the world; and may not this apply to a larger body?" He believed secrecy promoted respect for the Senate. One of the big issues in the Senate at the time was the Judiciary Act of 1789, which established the federal court system. Wingate served on the committee that drafted the bill. Wingate voted against it, although it passed. He felt it left too much for the state courts to decide.

Wingate lost his bid for re-election to the Senate in 1792 but won a seat in the United States House of Representatives, where he served from March 4, 1793, to March 3, 1795.

Wingate lost his re-election bid in 1794. He then served in the State House of Representatives until 1798, when he became an Associate Justice of the New Hampshire Supreme Court, serving until 1808. Theophilus Parsons, a jurist who served with Wingate, said this about him, "It was of great importance that your judge Wingate forms a correct opinion before he pronounces it- for after that, law, reason, and authority will be unavailing."

When Wingate died on March 7, 1838, he was the oldest graduate of Harvard and the last surviving member of the first United States Congress. His wife, Eunice, lived past 100 and is reported to have worn her wedding dress to her 100th birthday party. They are both buried in Stratham Cemetery.

Grave of Paine Wingate

Sources

Books, Magazines, Journals, Files:

Alexander, Edward P. *Revolutionary Conservative: James Duane of New York*. New York: Ams Press, 1978.

Anthony, Katharine Susan. *First Lady of the Revolution; The Life of Mercy Otis Warren*. Port Washington, N.Y.: Kennikat Press, 1972.

Appleby, Joyce. *Inheriting the Revolution: The First Generation of Americans*. Cambridge, Massachusetts: Harvard University Press, 2000.

Atkinson, Rick. *The British Are Coming: The War for America, Lexington to Princeton, 1775-1777*. New York: Henry Holt & Co. 2019.

Bordewich, Fergus M. *The First Congress: How James Madison, George Washington, and a Group of Extraordinary Men Invented the Government*. New York: Simon and Schuster Paperbacks, 2016.

Boudreau, George W. *Independence: A Guide to Historic Philadelphia*. Yardley, Pennsylvania: Westholme Publishing, LLC. 2012.

Bowen, Catherine Drinker. *Miracle at Philadelphia: The Story of the Constitutional Convention May to September 1787*. Boston, Massachusetts: Little, Brown & Company, 1966.

Breen, T.H, *George Washington's Journey: The President Forges a New Nation*. New York: Simon & Schuster. 2016.

Brookhiser, Richard. *Gentleman Revolutionary: Gouverneur Morris The Rake Who Wrote the Constitution*. New York: Free Press, 2003.

————. *John Marshall: The Man Who Made the Supreme Court*. New York: Basic Books. 2018.

Brush, Edward Hale. *Rufus King and His Times*. New York: N.L. Brown, 1926.

Chadwick, Bruce. I Am Murdered: *George Wythe, Thomas Jefferson, and the Killing That Shocked a New Nation*. Hoboken, New Jersey: John Wiley & Sons, 2009.

Chambers, II, John Whiteclay. *The Oxford Companion to American Military History*. Oxford: Oxford University Press, 1999.

Commager, Henry Steele & Richard B. Morris. *The Spirit of 'Seventy-Six: The Story of the American Revolution as Told by Participants*. New York: Harper & Rowe, 1967.

Cole, Ryan. *Light-Horse Harry Lee: The Rise and Fall of a Revolutionary Hero*. Washington, D.C.: Regnery History. 2019.

Conlin, Joseph R. *The Morrow Book of Quotations in American History*. New York: William Morrow and Company, Inc., 1984.

Daniels, Jonathan. *Ordeal of Ambition*. Garden City, New York: Doubleday & Company, Inc., 1970.

Dann, John C. *The Revolution Remembered: Eyewitness Accounts of the War for Independence*. Chicago: University of Chicago Press, 1980.

DeRose, Chris. *Founding Rivals: Madison vs. Monroe: The Bill of Rights and the Election that Saved a Nation*. New York: MJF Books, 2011.

Drury, Bob & Tom Clavin. *Valley Forge*. New York: Simon & Schuster. 2018.

Ellis, Joseph J. *Revolutionary Summer: The Birth of American Independence*. New York: Alfred A. Knopf, 2013.

———. *The Quartet: Orchestrating the Second American Revolution, 1783-1789*. New York: Alfred A. Knopf, 2015.

———. *His Excellency: George Washington*. New York: Alfred A. Knopf, 2004.

Flexner, James Thomas. *George Washington in the American Revolution, 1775-1783*. Boston: Little, Brown & Company, 1967.

Flower, Lenore Embick. "Visit of President George Washington to Carlisle, 1794." Carlisle, Pennsylvania: The Hamilton Library and Cumberland County Historical Society, 1932.

Gerlach, Don R. *Proud Patriot: Philip Schuyler and the War of Independence, 1775-1783*. Syracuse, N.Y.: Syracuse University Press, 1987.

Goodrich, Charles A. *Lives of the Signers of the Declaration of Independence*. Charlotteville, N.Y.: SamHar Press, 1976.

Griffith, IV, William R. *The Battle of Lake George: England's First Triumph in the French and Indian War*. Charleston, South Carolina: The History Press, 2016.

Grossman, Mark. *Encyclopedia of the Continental Congress*. Armenia, New York: Grey House Publishing, 2015.

Hamilton, Edward P. *Fort Ticonderoga: Key to a Continent*. Boston: Little, Brown & Company, 1964.

Isenberg, Nancy. *Fallen Founder: The Life of Aaron Burr*. New York: Penguin Group, 2007.

Kennedy, Roger G. *Burr, Hamilton, and Jefferson: A Study in Character*. New York: Oxford University Press, 1999.

Kiernan, Denise & Joseph D'Agnese. *Signing Their Lives Away: The Fame and Misfortune of the Men Who Signed the Declaration of Independence*. Philadelphia: Quirk Books, 2008.

———. *Signing Their Rights Away: The Fame and Misfortune of the Men Who Signed the United States Constitution*. Philadelphia: Quirk Books, 2011.

Klarman, Michael J. *The Framers' Coup: The Making of the United States Constitution*. New York: Oxford University Press, 2016.

Langguth, A. J. *Patriots*. New York: Simon and Schuster, 1988.

Larson, Edward J. *A Magnificent Catastrophe*. New York: Free Press, 2007.

Lee, Mike. *Written Out of History: The Forgotten Founders Who Fought Big Government*. New York: Penguin Books, 2017.

Lewis, James E., Jr., *The Burr Conspiracy: Uncovering the Story of an Early American Crisis*, Princeton: Princeton University Press, 2017.

Lockridge, Ross Franklin. *The Harrisons*. 1941.

Lomask, Milton. *Aaron Burr: The Years from Princeton to Vice President, 1756-1805*. New York: Farrar Straus Giroux, 1979.

Lossing, Benson J. *Pictorial Field Book of the Revolution*. New York: Harper Brothers. 1851.

SOURCES

Maier, Pauline. *American Scripture: Making the Declaration of Independence.* New York: Alfred A. Knopf, Inc., 1997.

McCullough, David. *John Adams.* New York: Simon & Schuster, 2002.

Meltzer, Brad & Josh Mensch. *The First Conspiracy: The Secret Plot to Kill George Washington.* New York: Flat Iron Books. 2018.

Middlekauff, Robert. *The Glorious Cause: The American Revolution, 1763-1789.* Oxford: Oxford University Press, 2005.

Miller, Jr., Arthur P. & Marjorie L. Miller. *Pennsylvania Battlefields and Military Landmarks.* Mechanicsburg, Pennsylvania: Stackpole Books, 2000.

Millett, Allan R. & Peter Maslowski. *For the Common Defense: A Military History of the United States of America.* New York: The Free Press, 1984.

Moore, Charles. *The Family Life of George Washington.* New York: Houghton Mifflin, 1926.

Nagel, Paul C. *The Lees of Virginia: Seven Generations of an American Family.* Oxford: Oxford University Press, 1990.

O'Connell, Robert L. *Revolutionary: George Washington at War.* New York: Random House. 2019.

Racove, Jack N. *Revolutionaries: A New History of the Invention of America.* New York: Houghton Mifflin Harcourt, 2011.

Raphael, Ray. Founding Myths: *Stories That Hide Our Patriotic Past.* New York: MJF Books, 2004.

Rossiter, Clinton. *1787 The Grand Convention.* New York: The Macmillan Company, 1966.

Seymour, Joseph. *The Pennsylvania Associators, 1747-1777.* Yardley, Pennsylvania: Westholme Publishing, LLC. 2012.

Schweikart, Larry & Michael Allen. *A Patriot's History of the United States from Columbus's Great Discovery to the War on Terror.* New York: Penguin, 2004.

Sharp, Arthur G. *Not Your Father's Founders.* Avon, Massachusetts: Adams Media, 2012.

Stahr, Walter. *John Jay: Founding Father.* New York: Diversion Books, 2017.

Taafee, Stephen R. *The Philadelphia Campaign, 1777-1778.* Lawrence, Kansas: University of Kansas Press, 2003.

Tinkcom, Harry Marlin, *The Republicans and the Federalists in Pennsylvania, 1790-1801.* Harrisburg, Pennsylvania: Pennsylvania Historical and Museum Commission. 1950.

Ward, Matthew C. *Breaking the Backcountry: The Seven Years' War in Virginia and Pennsylvania, 1754-1765.* Pittsburgh, Pennsylvania: University of Pittsburgh Press, 2003.

Weisberger, Bernard A. *America Afire: Jefferson, Adams, and the Revolutionary Election of 1800.* New York: HarperCollins, 2000.

Wood, Gordon S. *The Radicalism of the American Revolution.* New York: Vintage Books, 1993.

———. *Empire of Liberty: A History of the Early Republic, 1789-1815.* New York: Penguin Books, 2004.

———. *Revolutionary Characters: What Made the Founders Different.* New York: Penguin Books, 2006.

————. *The Americanization of Benjamin Franklin*. Oxford: Oxford University Press, 2009.

Wright, Benjamin F. *The Federalist: The Famous Papers on the Principles of American Government: Alexander Hamilton, James Madison, John Jay*. New York: Metro Books, 2002.

Zobel, Hiller B. *The Boston Massacre*. New York: W. W. Norton & Company, 1970.

Video Resources:

Guelzo, Allen C. The Great Courses: *America's Founding Fathers* (Course N. 8525). Chantilly, Virginia: The Teaching Company, 2017.

Online Resources:

Archives.gov – for information on the Constitutional Convention.

CauseofLiberty.blogspot.com – for information on Daniel Carroll.

ColonialHall.com – for information about the signers of the Declaration of Independence.

DSDI1776.com – for information on many Founders.

FamousAmericans.net – for information on many Founders.

FindaGrave.com – for burial information, vital statistics and obituaries.

FirstLadies.org – for information on Abigail Adams.

Newspapers.com – Hundreds of newspaper articles were accessed—too numerous to mention here.

NPS.gov – for information on various park sites.

TeachingAmericanHistory.com – for information on Charles Pinckney and George Wythe.

TheHistoryJunkie.com – for information on multiple Founders.

USHistory.org – for information on multiple Founders.

Wikipedia.com – for general historical information.

Index

INDEX

www.ingramcontent.com/pod-product-compliance
Lightning Source LLC
Chambersburg PA
CBHW011802040426
42449CB00016B/3464

9 798888 192122